Email Etiquette for Business Success

Use Emotional Intelligence to communicate effectively in the business world

Jeanne M. Fraser

Prepared for Kindle by
Masked Man Media
Galloway, Ohio
www.maskedmanmedia.com

Dedicated to my wonderful, kind, generous and loving
family and to
all the fabulous people
who spend a lot of time
communicating via email.

"Two monologues do not make a dialogue."
Jeff Daly

**"The relationship is the communication bridge between
people."**
Alfred Kadushin

Introduction

"In a man's letters his soul lies naked."
Samuel Johnson

My girlfriend Judith was one of the most interesting people I have ever met. She was incredibly well read and had a lifetime of experiences she shared with me. I talked to Judy over the phone at least twice a week and I always left the conversation learning something new or looking at something from a different perspective. I told Judy she needed to write a book and she said that putting words down on paper revealed too much of one's soul. Judy died in March of 2010 and I miss her dearly. I wish I did have some of Judy's soul captured in her writing.

I do believe to some extent that we bare part of our soul in our writing and that the words one puts down on paper or in an email have a life of their own. Emails have a way of landing up in some repository in the sky and may be circulating long after one has moved on. So, it is particularly important to pay attention to what one communicates in emails

The email phenomenon has taken us by storm and these days more than 90% of our communication is via email. We have had to join the email super highway without slowing down to consider the rules of the road. We are forced to stop sometime and pay the toll for haste, the forward and the 'reply to all' button.   Joseph Priestley said "The more elaborate our means of communication, the less we communicate" Communication is the key to developing relationships and is a key skill in the business world.   If we cannot communicate effectively we can not sell our ideas, let people know what we want or make any significant impact on the business.

"Regardless of the changes in technology, the market for well-crafted messages will always have an audience."
Steve Burnett.

Here's to you!

Emotional Intelligence(EI) - the key to your success

I want to share a little information on the significance of EI so that you understand its importance and the value to you.

Our success in life is to a large extent based on our ability to deal with people and manage ourselves. About 80% of our success is attributable to Emotional Intelligence and about 20% to cognitive intelligence. So if your IQ does not come near that of Einstein, take heart, there is more to success and life than scoring well on tests.

Emotional Intelligence is the ability to recognize and be aware of our own emotions and those of others. To use that awareness, to manage ourselves and our relationships with others.

Read on to find out how you can use Emotional Intelligence to communicate in the business world to get results that will help YOU be successful. Communicating effectively via email is just one facet of your brilliance, one facet of the diamond that you are.

Chapter I - Emotional Intelligence and Good Manners - (Managing self)

"Knowing a great deal is not the same as being smart; intelligence is not information alone but also judgment, the manner in which information is collected and used."
Dr. Carl Sagan – American Astronomer, Writer and Scientist, 1934-1996.

"Manners are a sensitive awareness of the feelings of others. If you have that awareness, you have good manners, no matter what fork you use."
Emily Post – American authority on social behavior – 1872-1960

These are two of my favorite quotes on manners. Knowledge does not make you smart, in fact, IQ is only a fraction of what it takes to be successful. Some studies show that having superior interpersonal and intrapersonal skills can contribute up to 80% of a person's ability to succeed on the job and in life.

I believe that we can not significantly change the IQ we are born with but that we can grow other areas of our intelligence significantly. Specifically, the way we relate with others.

Howard Gartner introduced the concept of eight multiple intelligences.

1. Verbal /Linguistic
2. Logical/Mathematical
3. Musical
4. Visual
5. Bodily /Kinesthetic
6. Naturalistic
7. Interpersonal
8. Intrapersonal

The first two **(verbal/linguistic, logical/ mathematical)** deal with cognitive intelligence, which is the ability to read, write, comprehend, do mathematics, etc. (Albert Einstein had high cognitive intelligence.)

Musical intelligence deals with those individuals who are exceptionally gifted in the art of music. My husband can hear a song once and play it on the piano by ear. My daughter can hear a song, immediately pick out the harmony, memorize the words and sing the song so beautifully that it brings tears to my eyes.

Visual intelligence is the ability to be able to look at a scene and recreate it on paper or some other medium, to see a block of stone and visualize the statue that could be carved out of it. Michael Angelo had the monopoly on this intelligence.

Bodily/Kinesthetic intelligence is the ability to fine tune our bodies to perform all kinds of athletic feats. (Olympic athletes have honed their bodily intelligence)

Naturalistic intelligence is the ability to detect very small changes in the environment. A girlfriend of mine can pick out a slight change in my kitchen and sometimes I move some plates around that are displayed just to see if she would notice and she does. I have 57 plates displayed and they are all blue and white.

Emotional Intelligence deals with the last two intelligences – **intrapersonal and interpersonal**. Dealing with yourself and dealing with others. Emotional Intelligence is a four quadrant model; simply put, it is understanding yourself, understanding others, managing your self and managing/relating to others.

Recognizing that the only person you can really control is yourself is a powerful milestone in the maturity journey.

So what does that have to do with email etiquette?

In the business world, we deal with large populations of people we don't know, we may not like or we may not agree with.   Using good manners is a way to develop better relationships, to have a difference of opinion without being offensive and to be able to influence people who you may not ever get to meet face to face.

Margaret Mead, a famous American anthropologist said that manners are a way of dealing with people you don't agree with or like.

The Jeanne Fraser definition of Leadership is: **The ability to engage the hearts and minds of your team to collaborate and innovate.** To be a leader you must develop your emotional intelligence, engage the hearts and minds of your tribe and exhibit good manners.

It costs nothing to say "please" and "thank you" and yet, you will be amazed at how many people in the business world make requests without employing their manners. It would be just as rude to sit across a table with a business associate or customer and say "pass the butter". When saying please in an email, it is not cool to abbreviate the word to "pls". It does not take but one extra second to add three vowels to the word.

"Thank you" is an extremely underutilized phrase in the English language. It is a powerful duo of words and it pays your way forward. Please use it! It is not cool to say "thanks" , "tx", "TU" or "thank U". It does not take much more effort to write "Thank You" and to use the person's name after the 'Thank You'. A "thx" at the bottom of the email indicates to me that what I did for the other person was not appreciated and that it was not even worthy of a few extra seconds of their time.

When using instant messaging, it is the norm to use abbreviations. However, not everyone understands all the abbreviations. Most of us work in a global environment and it is difficult enough to communicate when using correct English. Please don't interject instant messaging abbreviations into your emails unless it is with a personal friend that you are communicating with and one that is familiar with your abbreviations and acronyms. TTFN, LOL, TTYL, TU, BTW, BFF, OIC!

Another breach of etiquette in the email world is not responding to an associate or customer when they send you an email. I have found that for some reason when most people obtain their executive stripes, they lose their manners . Executives hide behind the "I am too important to respond to your email" persona.   I think this is a breach of etiquette. When executives don't respond to emails that they receive from employees who are below them in the hierarchy the perception they create is that do not care. Executives in general have administrative support and they should make every effort to connect with the people in their organization. When you find an executive that has excellent intrapersonal and interpersonal skills, you generally find an organization that is effective, has high morale and productivity. Always respond to someone even if you have to say NO to what they are asking for or if all your response consists of is a simple "thank you." Remember, your response or lack of response speaks volumes about who you really are. How do you want to come across to your customer, your management, your team?

Chapter II - The Subject Line - (managing self)

A few months ago, I received an email from someone whose name I did not recognize, with a subject line of "Can't wait to catch up with you". At first glance, the subject is benign and should not cause any alarm. But, if you, like me get a bunch of spam it looks like just another attempt for some dating or mating organization trying to solicit business. These emails are tawdry and become increasingly annoying. That one made it into the virtual trash bin. Then a few days later, I got an email from the same person with a subject line of FW: Can't wait to catch up with you. That email joined its predecessor. I continued to ignore the emails from this person until finally the subject line read, "Follow up from our CCT meeting in June."

The sender, Susan, happened to be a wonderful person I met at a coaching community meeting. When I met her, I was told her married name, but her emails had her maiden name, so I did not recognize it. and I would have blocked her permanently from my mail if I did not recognize her name. I was introduced to her by her married name and her email had her maiden name. Subsequently, we have connected and we both would have lost out if we did not connect initially due to a cryptic subject line.

Make your subject lines work for you and help the recipient respond appropriately. The subject line should indicate the topic and what action the recipient should take. Here are some effective subject lines:

Minutes of 1/15/2011 meeting – please note action items

Proposal you requested – please reply by 1/30/2011

Break through ideas – please rank by importance.

FYI only – No action required.

I strongly advocate using a person's name in the salutation but please don't use it in the subject line as it is inappropriate and considered rude especially if the recipient of the email is your business superior. In the business world when sending a note to multiple individuals, it may not be possible to use a person's name in the subject line but if you are communicating with just one person, use the person's name when it makes sense.

Jeanne, For your information only.

Jeanne, FYI only, No action required.

Jeanne Please read in preparation for the XYZ meeting.

Jeanne, please respond by Date

Jeanne, Your input please ?.

When I open my email in-box, I scan through the scores of emails I receive daily and delete a bunch of them before I attempt to open any of them. I delete the emails if I don't trust the source or if the subject line reads Fw: Fw: Fw: Fw Fw.

When an email is replied to repeatedly, it carries the subject line of the original note. You may want to consider changing or updating the subject line if the context of your most current note has changed from the original subject line. Consider and craft your subject lines to intrigue, inform and get the response you require.

Chapter III -The Salutation (relating to others)

What's in a name?

Dale Carnegie said that a person's name is the sweetest and most important sound in any language.   People love the sound of their own name.   Have you been in a meeting where the presenter uses your name to give you credit or to indicate that you are the contact person for a certain project? I bet that even if you were day dreaming, you heard your name and it got your attention.

If you are working at an office and you see a co-worker for the first time that day, even if you are not the most extroverted person in the world, you will probably say hello and greet them by their name.

A name gives us our individual identity. Our name is so much a part of who we are that we can not separate it from our hearts and emotions. It is who we are and identifies us as part of society.

When we receive a name at birth, we become part of society and have tacit membership in all the rights, privileges and norms of a particular culture. In turn, we are required to honor that membership and live up to our part of the intimated contract.

Prisoners in Western cultures are stripped of their names and all the implied privileges that come with it. They are given a number instead. This implies that they are no longer part of the society that used to recognize them as individuals. They have broken the tacit agreement and as a result, they have forfeited the advantage of being called by their given name.

People are given a name on the day they are born and unless they take legal action to have it changed, they keep their first name until they die.

Some famous African Americans in the sixties changed their names to identify with other societies because they believed they had been wronged or let down by the society in which they lived. It is not unusual today for African Americans to have Muslim or "African" names. (Please note that there are other reasons for persons changing their names – to connect with their culture, to honor their heritage or to identify with their ancestors. The example above is used to illustrate the significance of names in society.)

Sometimes I get calls from telemarketers who I do declare have a spycam in my home because it never fails that just when we are about to sit down to a family meal, they call asking for G Ann Fraser! Not only is the call an intrusion on my family time, a waste of my time, but they get my name wrong! They do not make a sale.

A faux pas just as grievous as not using a person's name correctly, is to misspell it. Take the time to find out how a person spells their name; is it Kathy with a 'K' or Cathy with a 'C'?

Don't assume intimacy by calling someone a diminutive of their name or use a familiar Charlie for Charles, Dick for Richard, Bill for William, Vicki for Victoria or Jim or Jimmy for James, unless the person specifically gives you permission to do so. In Victorian England and even in some cultures today, the use of a person's first name is only permissible with explicit permission. It denotes an intimacy one does not have upon first acquaintance

In the Anglo-Saxon world (Britain, USA, Canada, Australia, New Zealand), calling someone by their surname is regarded as formal and respectful, whereas use of a first name or Christian name is regarded as familiar and friendly. Most people, especially the younger generation (gen x) prefer to use a person's first name even if they are dealing with their superiors in the corporate hierarchy.

In Japan, a family name is typically used when addressing someone followed by the title 'san'. Using a person's last name without a title is considered rude and disrespectful even in informal situations. The use of given(first) names are restricted and used by older people when addressing someone younger or in very informal situations. Note: It is perfectly acceptable to use someone's given(first) name with their permission.

In Spain, a person's first name is followed by two family names. The first is the surname of the father and the second name is the surname of the mother.

The accepted practice is to use a person's first name and the first surname only. The full name (both surnames) is used only in legal and formal documentation.

In the US, using a person's first name is a common practice in business and is expected. So, use it properly, spell it correctly and when in doubt, ask the person how they would like to be addressed.

When communicating with someone via email, please use his or her name in the salutation. It is the first step to creating a connection with the individual, it honors them and characterizes you as a person who has taken the time to recognize the individual as someone who matters, someone who is worthy of being addressed by their name.

Chapter IV - The body of the email (managing self/relating to others)

"Water, water everywhere but not a drop to drink"

In our virtual world today, there is "data, data every where but we can not stop to think". It is almost impossible to keep up with all the information that we are faced with every day. So how do you get your message across succinctly? Simplify! Make your message clear and consistent. Remember that communicating is a two way dialogue. What you say must be heard and heard in the manner you want your message to be interpreted.

A good rule of thumb is to cover the who, what, when, where, why and how in an email. I recently received an email, followed by another and another because the author was hasty and failed to provide all the information the first time. This carelessness gives the recipient an unfavorable impression of the sender. One assumes that the person doesn't have their act together and therefore does not deserve to be taken too seriously. It is inconsiderate and causes the recipient to have to open several pieces of mail to get the whole picture. My grandmother always said that haste makes waste and haste in this example wastes not only the sender's but the recipient's time as well.

Keep the information as brief and concise as possible. If you work for a corporation or business enterprise, chances are that you use email as the primary form of communication. People respond to emails that are heart centered, easy to read, of interest to them, clear in their instruction and have a specific request and expected deadline. Before you send an email, to honor the recipient, take the time to reread your email for accuracy. We think faster than we can type and sometimes we replace nouns with pronouns that lead to confusion. For example: The boy ran towards the man. He yelled out to him to stop. (It is not clear in the second sentence whether the boy or the man yelled – so for clarity, use the noun 'boy' or 'man" instead of the pronouns he or him.).

Provide hyperlinks in an email if you are referring to information available on a Web site. If you make the task easier for the reader, you are more likely to get a faster and more accurate response.

Use the formatting functions available to you in your email application. If you want to call attention to a particular instruction or question, do not hesitate to highlight it.

People in general do not like reading reams of information so please keep your email brief.   Use bullets if the order does not matter and use a numbered list if the order has significance.

Tell the recipient the purpose of your email right up front. Give them all the facts as concisely as possible, then at the end, reiterate what you want the recipient to do. Again, please use your manners.

Web marketing research indicates that

messages have the most impact

If the text is extended only

to the middle of a page.

It is considered the easiest form

for the recipient to read and digest

the information quickly.

- Bullets are another excellent
- way to separate your thoughts
- and to highlight salient points.
- Don't be afraid to use bullets.

(Again, if the order does not matter.)

Always use spell check. We are critical creatures and are drawn to mistakes even if 99% of the email is correct. When viewing a presentation, everyone hones in on an incorrect spelling or a typographical error. When you have limited time to get your message across and hold someone's attention you don't want them focusing on a misspelled word instead of your message. There is no excuse for sending out an email without using the spell check function. Most email software now has auto-spell checker, correcting as you go.

If you are asking the recipient to take some action, do not give them too much time to respond unless your request requires a huge expenditure of time. For most requests, a week should be enough. If you give someone two weeks to respond, chances are that the person will put it off for a couple of weeks because it does not generate a sense of urgency and will probably be forgotten or remain unanswered.

Please use your manners in an email; it reflects on who you are and how well you were raised.   Politeness is not an option; it is a requirement in the business world.

Connecting with people and establishing relationships is critical to business success.   Use each email as an opportunity to connect with people on an emotional and intellectual level.

Chapter V - Your signature (Managing self)

Your signature lines must have all the pertinent information necessary to contact you. It should include your name, title, phone number and Web site (if applicable).

People tend to use email to broadcast their passion, their religion or their political leanings. It is not appropriate to use business emails as a forum to make religious or political statements, unless you work for a religious or political organization. These subjects are taboo; they tend to create an immediate barrier to communicating and create a huge rift into any possibility of developing a relationship with people. The business implications of imposing your religious beliefs and political passions via email are serious and are detrimental to your business.

I dislike opening emails from some people at work because they have included their pictures in the email and it takes forever to handle the email. If you are using your picture (which I personally endorse using as it gives the reader a sense of who you are), please be considerate and ensure that your picture is sized correctly. Please get the technical help you need to ensure that its inclusion does not slow down the opening of your email.

Chapter VI - When not to use email (managing yourself)

Do not use email if:

- You want to thank someone for extraordinary effort.
- You want to apologize for some significant infraction.
- You want to maintain the privacy of your message.
- You want to sell a radical idea.
- You have to deliver bad news.

Chapter VII - The Golden Rule - (managing yourself)

The golden rule is to do unto others as you would have them do unto you. It is very important in the business world and in general to allow people to save face.

If someone makes a mistake in an email and they have copied several people, the kindest thing to do would be to reply only to the sender and make them aware of the mistake. It is not professional to reply to everyone and embarrass the sender. It may make you feel superior or smart but in reality it makes you look insensitive.

You don't want to be copied on every single email so don't do it to others. If someone sends out an email and all you want to say is thank you to the person, it is unnecessary to copy everyone on the email. It is important to be respectful of people's time. The exception here is if you are the manager of the person and want to publicly thank the sender and your thanking the sender publicly would mean something to everyone who receives the email.

If you are forwarding mail that was forwarded to you, unless the history of all the forwards has some significance, make the effort to delete all the unnecessary information and send on only the information that is pertinent.

Always respond to an email if it requires a response. Ignoring an email is just as rude as ignoring someone who greets you in the hallway.   Sometimes just a simple "thank you" to let the person know you received the email will suffice. At the least, let the recipient know you will respond with specific details at a later date if you cannot respond immediately and then follow through with your promise. Integrity is doing what you say you will do.

Chapter VIII - Dealing with contentious situations (managing yourself)

"Anger is an acid that can do more harm to the vessel in which it is stored than to anything on which it is poured."
Mark Twain.

"For every minute you remain angry, you give up sixty seconds of peace of mind."
Ralph Waldo Emerson.

"He who angers you conquers you."
Elizabeth Kenny.

A key component of being emotionally intelligent is to recognize your anger and be aware of how you deal with it.

I was recently copied on an email that was sent to numerous people informing me of an auction that was to take place to dispose of a friend's estate. The step-daughter of the deceased didn't use good judgment and questioned the integrity of the executor of the will. The daughter of the executor of the will sent back a scathing reply to everyone on the copy list attacking the grammar, style and intent of the step- daughter and ardently defended the character and integrity of her mother, the executor. Unfortunately the grammar of the scathing reply left something to be desired as well. This became an all out email war; several of the people copied on the note decided to help by getting involved with sage advice and their opinions. This generated another slew of emails and became ridiculous. Even though I deleted all further emails that kept going back and forth, each time I received an email on this subject, it triggered a sense of turmoil and uneasiness which I felt in the pit of my stomach. One thoughtless email generated a barrage of angry responses and negative feelings. We have a responsibility to ourselves and others to avoid generating negativity.

Words, once spoken cannot be taken back. Words once written live on forever.   It reminds me of the story that has been circulating on the internet in which a father makes his son hammer a nail into a fence every time he says something hurtful. The son turns over a new leaf and is then instructed to remove the nail form the fence whenever he does a kind act. Over time he removes all the nails one by one but eventually realizes that the fence is now riddled with holes.

"Holding on to anger is like grasping a hot coal with the intent of throwing it at someone else; you are the one who gets burned."

OR

"Holding on to anger is like drinking poison and expecting the other person to die."
Buddha

If you are angry or upset, by a certain piece of correspondence then you should write out the reply but don't mail it until you have had a chance to sleep on it and review it from a different emotional platform. My suggestion is NOT to write the email at all because it is very easy to hit the SEND button in a moment of emotional stress and you will leave a gaping hole in the proverbial fence, even if you later retract your words. A good alternative is to write your response the old fashioned way with pen and paper or write the email to yourself so that when you read it the next day you could rethink your response in a calmer frame of mind. It is therapeutic and will prevent you form responding to another with anger.

Email is NOT a vehicle for your anger, take a moment, take a deep breath and let it go. **Willard Gaylin** said that Expressing Anger is a form of public littering! Email is a public forum – don't litter.

Chapter IX – STOP before you hit SEND (managing yourself)

Have you:

- Considered who should be copied on the email?
- Used and spelled the recipient's name correctly?
- Used the opportunity to connect with the recipient?
- Communicated the who, what, when, where, why and how?
- Asked for what you want clearly and politely?
- Considered the reaction of the recipient?
- Reread your email for clarity and correct grammar?
- Used the format function to make your email easily readable?

Chapter X - Instant Messaging (managing yourself)

I feel compelled to address Instant Messaging, as it is such a common part of our daily lives, albeit imposing.

Instant Messaging(IM) is the real-time transmission of a text-based message over a computer that uses software to instantly display the message in a window on the screen of the recipient.

An instant message is an interruption that borders on rudeness. It is incredibly impolite to send an instant message asking a question without checking with the recipient if it is a good time to start a chat using instant messaging.

An instant message says to me "My need to have an instant response is greater than your need to concentrate on what you are doing right now"

Unlike an IM, an email does not interrupt or disrupt us while we are in the midst of serious thought or creativity. An email allows us to graciously receive the message at our convenience.

Instant messaging among the members of a close team or someone you know really well is acceptable if that is the protocol established by you and the team.

The long and the short of it is to keep instant messaging down to a minimum. Just because you have the capability/right to send an instant message, does not make it the right thing to do. Remember the Golden rule, Do unto others as you would have them do unto you.

When instant messaging is appropriate in the business world:

- When you are on a conference call and you want to share information that is pertinent to the people on the call.
- When you are on a telephone call and need to get information to someone immediately OR if you need to reach someone urgently and they are on a call.
- When you are trying to locate a team member to join a call.
- When you are working on a team and you have agreed that instant messaging is an acceptable way to collaborate.

- When you want to provide a speaker/team member with information that is being requested by the audience.

Please do not initiate an Instant message if:

- You don't have to have a response instantly (an email will be appropriate).
- When you are communicating with someone higher in the chain of command.
- When what you have to say has very little importance to the recipient.
- You have a lot of information to share
- You want to show appreciation
- You want to have a record of the communication
- You have any doubt about whether to send the instant message.   Listen to your inner voice.

The origin of the words 'please' and 'thank You'

I am fascinated with etymology and want to share with you, the origin of the words 'please' and 'thank you'. 'Please' originated in English in the early 14 th century and it meant "to be agreeable," a similar word in French is ' plaisir' which means 'to please. In Latin, the word 'placere' means to be acceptable, be liked or to be approved. The imperative use (e.g. please do this), was first recorded 1620s, was probably an abbreviation of " if it pleases you". So when we say "Please sit down" it is short for "may it please you to sit down or sit down if it pleases you".

Thank you is a conventional expression of gratitude. It originated from English. Prior to 900, the word 'thank' meant a favorable thought, goodwill or gratitude. In old English, the word was 'thanc' or 'thancian' which translated to thought or thoughtfulness.

Message from Jeanne Fraser

Time is a precious commodity so thank you for choosing to spend it reading this eBook. I hope you found the content worthy of your time and that you will put the information to good use.

I wish for you a life filled with joy, gratitude and abundance.   If you have any ideas or additional email etiquette hints and tips not covered here, please do not hesitate to send them to me. I would love to hear from you.

Love and blessings,

Jeanne Fraser